· A · PRACTICAL · GUIDE · FOR · TEACHERS ·

ASSIGNMENTS IN FOOD

Marjorie Keedy

Blackie

British Library Cataloguing in Publication Data

Keedy, Marjorie
  Assignments in food: a practical guide
  for teachers.
  1. Cookery—Questions & answers
  I. Title
  641.5'076

  ISBN 0-216-92423-5

Blackie & Son Ltd
Bishopbriggs Glasgow G64 2NZ
7 Leicester Place London WC2H 7BP

Printed in Great Britain by Thomson Litho Ltd., East Kilbride, Scotland

INTRODUCTION

This book has been compiled with a view to helping teachers who are involved in teaching practical assignments in Home Economics: Food in the GCSE and Standard Grade examinations.

The book contains 40 planned assignments, each with comprehensive Teacher's Notes, an Index explaining the range of skills and knowledge anticipated from the assignments, plus a sample Pupil's Recording Chart and a Teacher's Evaluation Chart both of which may be photocopied free of charge. The Pupil's Recording Chart is a personal evaluation which should be retained by each student in a folder.

The ability to investigate, analyse and evaluate rather than just cook is of the essence in the National Criteria, and these assignments comply with those requirements. Equally, the needs of NACNE, COMA and the GCSE assessment objectives have been considered and the common themes appropriate to each have been noted in the Index. The terminology used should be familiar, but this should not prevent the teacher simplifying or explaining odd words for use with younger students if necessary.

All the assignments have been carefully selected to give as wide a cross section of work as possible. Each one can be adapted by the teacher to accommodate different age ranges and abilities. Obviously one cannot hope to work through all 40 assignments in the last two years of an examination course, therefore it is important that they can be used further down the school, so that all pupils become *au fait* with the type of questions they can expect to meet in the final term.

It would be disappointing for both pupils and staff if practical lessons lost the very pleasant end products to which all have become accustomed, so each assignment involves cooking skills as well as investigative ones so that there is something to take home at the end of the day or to sample in class. I am sure that this will be appreciated by those who anticipate problems in getting parents to provide ingredients for experimental purposes with nothing to show for their money. In these exercises little food is deliberately spoiled.

While all assignments can be used as they stand, there is no reason why the teacher should not adapt or modify them to suit the requirements of the students, food availability, time and cost. Whenever possible it has been suggested that students should work in small groups in order to avoid tedious repetition of processes. For example, where an assignment involves 3 different processes using one type of food, it has been suggested that students should work in groups of 3, each working on one process and then collating the information obtained.

Since very few schools will allow classes any extra time for assignments it is inevitable that groups of students may be involved in research, practical and follow-up work at the same time. In order to give those doing practical work enough space to operate efficiently and safely, it would be beneficial to organise a separate, quiet resource area where those doing planning and follow-up projects can work.

Resource areas are very important if students are to be able to research at their own pace within the group situation, and ideally they should be as striking as possible to attract the less academic student. Most teachers will have their own approaches to resource centres and these will be governed by cost and space. At one end of the scale, simple home-made posters and blackboard work may suffice, but well-chosen textbooks, commercial leaflets and wall charts can be of great value, while food tables are essential. For those with access to computers, there is some excellent software on the market and this can often be hired from the local authority's own resource centre. Contact with a Home Economics Adviser can be most productive when a new resource area is being set up, and some areas are building up banks of information which can be borrowed on a short-term basis. This type of interaction between schools can mean frequent changes of scene to retain pupil interest without putting too heavy a burden on the teacher.

INDEX OF ASSIGNMENTS

ASSIGN-MENT NO	PAGE	TOPIC	KNOWLEDGE & SKILLS ANTICIPATED	COMMON THEMES (National Criteria)
7	14	Comparison of various brands of canned carrots	Evaluation of content of canned vegetables, e.g., quantity of liquid. Costing of each can once liquid has been removed. Comparison of canned carrots with fresh per pound. Nutritional value of canned veg.	2, 4, 5, 7
8	16	Steamed pudding made in pressure cooker and steamer	Steaming as a method of cooking. Pressure cooking. Creaming method of cake-making. Use of sponge mixture in meal-planning. Adaptation of recipes to make meal for 2 people.	3, 4, 6
9	18	Dishes using mince	Cost of mince—economy of time and money. Varieties of mince. Meal-planning using mince. Nutritional value of mince. Foreign cooking. Accompaniments and garnishes. Roux sauces. Herbs and spices. Pasta cooking.	1, 4, 5, 6
10	20	Fish—fillets versus whole fish	Classification of fish. Filleting and skinning of fish—waste element. Fish cooking—accompaniments and garnishes. Nutritional value of fish. Meal-planning with fish. Methods of cooking fish.	1, 2, 4, 6, 7
11	22	Creaming method using various veg margarines	Creaming method of cake-making. Correct choice of margarines, i.e., not low fat margarines. Appropriate cooking time for quantity of mixture. Oven temperatures. Variations on creaming method. Food value of veg margarines. Additives.	1, 2, 4, 5, 7

ASSIGN- MENT NO	PAGE	TOPIC	KNOWLEDGE & SKILLS ANTICIPATED	COMMON THEMES (National Criteria)
12	24	Alternative methods of sweetening used in creaming method	Creaming method of cake-making. Types of sugar available. Alternative methods of sweetening. Food value of sugar. Dangers of excess sugar consumption, i.e., diseases caused by sugar. Low sugar diets—diabetics. Artificial sweeteners.	1, 2, 4, 5
13	26	Yeast cookery	Preparation of bread. Use of dried yeast and ascorbic acid. Conditions required for development of yeast. Correct recipe and oven temperature. Kneading and shaping. Types of flour used in bread-making. Comparison of costs. Effect of salt, sugar, heat and cold on yeast. Nutritional value of bread.	4, 5
14	28	Sauce cooking—roux	Basic sauce theory and variation on recipe. Sweet and savoury sauces. Pouring, coating and panadas. Reasons for the use of sauces. Brown and white sauces. Hot and cold sauces.	1, 4, 5, 6
15	30	Textured Vegetable Protein in beefburgers	Construction of TVP. Food value of TVP. Use of TVP in conjunction with fresh meat. Vegetarian cookery. Low fat or fat-free diets. Low cost HBV protein meals. Use in under-nourished societies. Long-term food storage.	2, 3, 4, 5, 7
16	32	Cooking for one	Adaptation of recipe for one person. Nutritional value of meats for e.g: a pensioners b widows/widowers c students	2, 3, 4, 5, 6, 7

ASSIGN-MENT NO	PAGE	TOPIC	KNOWLEDGE & SKILLS ANTICIPATED	COMMON THEMES (National Criteria)
17	34	Mashed potato	Ability to choose correct type for mashing. Method of cooking potato to conserve nutrients. Familiarity with utensils for mashing. Vegetable preparation showing awareness of need for reducing waste.	3, 4, 5, 6, 7
18	36	Scrambled eggs cooked in microwave	Properties of eggs. Knowledge of microwave cookery. Egg nutrition. Correct presentation and garnish. Costing of meal. Coagulation of protein.	3, 4, 5, 6
19	38	Melted chocolate in mousse	Use of double boiler. Correct melting of chocolate. Use of eggs in mousse. Food value of chocolate and mousse. Value of chocolate as emergency snack. Various shapings of chocolate. Decorative presentation.	2, 3, 4, 5, 6
20	40	Shortcrust pastry in food processor	Preparation of shortcrust pastry. Use of processor. Shaping and finishing of small pies. Comparative cost of bought and home-made pies.	2, 3, 4, 5, 6
21	42	Cheese in cookery. Pizza.	Nutritive value of cheese. Types of cheese, characteristics and origins. Preparation of pizza. Effect of heat on cheese. Production of cheese.	2, 4, 5, 6, 7
22	44	Toaster v grill	Use of electric toaster. Use of gas grill: use of electric grill. Types of bread suitable for toasting. Cost of electric toasters. Nutritive value of bread. Production of dextrin.	3, 4, 5, 6, 7
23	46	Baked egg custard	Properties of eggs. Use of Bain Marie. Cooking temperatures for egg custards. Egg custards in special diets. Coagulation of protein in custards. Digestion of egg custard. Fuel economy.	1, 2, 3, 4, 5, 6, 7

ASSIGN-MENT NO	PAGE	TOPIC	KNOWLEDGE & SKILLS ANTICIPATED	COMMON THEMES (National Criteria)
24	48	Coating fish for frying	Preparation of fish. Use of different coatings. Fats and oils for frying. Frying temperatures. Nutritive value of fried fish. Accompaniments and garnishes for fish. Choice of fish. Freshness of fish. Safety aspects of frying.	2, 3, 4, 5, 6, 7
25	50	Milk dishes	Nutritive value of milk. Types of milk and their properties. Milk production and cost. Effect of heat on milk. Milk processing. Milk products.	1, 2, 3, 5, 6
26	52	Yoghurt	Food value and cost. Home production of yoghurt. Yoghurt flavourings. History of yoghurt. Yoghurt in special diets. Experiments with yoghurt.	1, 2, 4, 5, 6, 7
27	54	Flaky pastry	Theory of preparation and ingredients. Shaping of sausage rolls. Comparative cost with shop pastry. Nutritional value of pastry. Uses in sweet and savoury dishes. Fats used in pastry—COMA.	2, 4, 5, 6, 7
28	56	Home-made mayonnaise	Use of blender. Use of hand whisk. Emulsification of eggs. Comparison between home-made and bought. Properties of eggs. Uses of mayonnaise. Safety in use of blender. Lower fat alternatives.	2, 3, 4, 5, 6, 7
29	58	Blanching	Reasons for blanching food. Methods of blanching. Foods for blanching. Theory of freezing. Freezer packaging.	2, 4, 6

ASSIGN-MENT NO	PAGE	TOPIC	KNOWLEDGE & SKILLS ANTICIPATED	COMMON THEMES (National Criteria)
30	60	Glazes	Theory of glazing fruit flans. Use of cornflour: use of arrowroot: use of Quick Jel. Food values of glazes. Lining a fluted flan ring. Preparation of sweet shortcrust pastry.	2, 4, 5, 6
31	62	Apple pie	Preparation of pastry. Lining and covering plate pie. Fruit preparation: peeler, grater, knife. Fruit cookery—stewing. Theory enzymic browning. Food value of pie. Finishing of pie.	2, 3, 4, 5, 6
32	64	Bread—packet v home-made	Chorleywood method. Yeast theory. Cooking temperatures. Shaping of bread. Cost of each type. Bread additives.	1, 2, 3, 4, 5, 6, 7
33	66	Cooking green vegetables	Nutritive value of brussels sprouts. Correct method of preparation. Correct method of cooking. Vitamin C loss. Use of bicarbonate of soda.	1, 2, 5, 6, 7
34	68	Meringues	Use of microwave. Properties of eggs. Use of whisk. Shaping of meringues. Economy in using up leftover egg whites. Seasonal cookery. Cake decoration. Comparison of results.	4, 5, 6
35	70	Egg custard v packet	Eggs as thickeners. Use of cornflour. Food value of custard. Protein coagulation. Cooking temperatures. Sugar content. Comparative prices. Curdling in egg custards. Digestion of protein. Egg custards in special diets. Use of double boiler.	1, 2, 3, 4, 5, 6

ASSIGN-MENT NO	PAGE	TOPIC	KNOWLEDGE & SKILLS ANTICIPATED	COMMON THEMES (National Criteria)
36	72	Browning microwave foods	Use of microwave. Use of browning dishes and agents. Comparison of results. Food value of foods browned. Scone preparation.	2, 3, 4, 5, 6
37	74	Toffee	Preparation of toffee. Sugar cooking temperatures. Use of sugar thermometer. Stages of brittleness. Testing for correct texture and firmness. Packaging for sale. Food value of toffee. Uses in cookery. Sugar related diseases.	1, 2, 3, 5 6, 7
38	76	Fresh white breadcrumbs	Use of blender. Use of grater. Use of food processor. Value of breadcrumbs in cooking. Gratin dishes. Comparison of raspings and breadcrumbs. Uses of breadcrumbs.	4, 5, 6
39	78	Baked beans	Cost of variously sized cans—economy. Food value of beans. Use in vegetarian diets. Versatility. Comparison of brands. Quantity of sauce and beans. Beans on the menu as a vegetable.	3, 5, 6, 7
40	80	Enzyme action on apples	Preparation of shortcrust pastry. Fruit preparation. Shaping of small fruit pies. Finishing small pies. Prevention of browning in cut apples. Enzyme action in other fruits and vegetables. Loss of nutrients from cut fruit.	4, 5, 6, 7

PUPIL'S RECORDING CHART

NAME _____ DATE _____

TASK _____

CHOICE _____

BRIEF DESCRIPTION OF HOW TASK WAS CARRIED OUT

_____

_____

_____

_____

EQUIPMENT USED _____

TIME **a** *PREPARATION* _____ **b** *COOKING* _____

OVEN TEMPERATURE GAS _____ *ELECTRICITY* _____

SERVING SUGGESTIONS _____

_____

_____

_____

_____

POSSIBILITY OF IMPROVEMENTS IN

a *METHOD OF WORKING* _____

_____

b *FINISHED RESULTS* _____

_____

COST OF FINISHED DISH/DISHES

_____

FOOD VALUES

Ingredient	Protein	Fat	Starch/sugar	Vitamins	Minerals

DO THE DISHES MEET WITH RECOMMENDED DIETARY GOALS?

_____

_____

COMMENTS TO INCLUDE POSSIBLE VARIATIONS

_____

_____

_____

_____

_____

_____

ASSESSMENT OF FINISHED RESULT _____

_____

TEACHER'S MARK _____

TEACHER'S EVALUATION CHART

ASSIGNMENT NO:

PUPIL'S NAME											
PREPARATION (Max. 5)											
CHOICE OF WORK i.e. DISHES CHOSEN TO COMPLETE ASSIGNMENT (Max. 8)											
MANIPULATIVE AND COOKING SKILLS SHOWN (Max. 10)											
OVEN CONTROL OR USE OF MECHANICAL/ELECTRICAL EQUIPMENT WHERE APPROPRIATE (Max. 6)											
METHOD OF WORK INCLUDING HYGIENE (Max. 10)											
PRESENTATION/AESTHETIC APPRECIATION (Max. 5)											
WRITTEN EVALUATION i.e. CHARTS (Max. 6)											
FOLLOW UP LESSON/ORAL EVALUATION (Max. 10)											
MINUS MARKS FOR INDIVIDUAL ASSISTANCE GIVEN IN ANY OF ABOVE AREAS (−10)											
TOTAL (Max. 60)											

ASSIGNMENTS IN FOOD

ASSIGNMENT 1

You are moving into a flat and looking for some kitchen utensils. You want to find out which piece of equipment would be best for making a whisked fatless sponge.

Compare and evaluate a range of mechanical and/or electrical equipment which would be appropriate for your purpose.

▶ ## PREPARATION

Suggested whisking equipment

> balloon whisk
> hand electric whisk
> rotary whisk
> food processor

Basic recipe

> 2 eggs
> 50 g castor sugar
> 50 g plain flour

▶ ## PRACTICAL

1 Prepare a sandwich cake tin of the correct size.
2 Pre-heat the oven to the appropriate temperature.
3 Using the above mixture prepare a basic jam sponge.
4 Prepare chart on which the following information can be recorded:
   a whisking time,
   b ease of use of each piece of equipment,
   c time taken to clean equipment,
   d finished appearance of cakes,
   e taste of cakes,
   f texture of cakes,
   g cost of equipment,
   h versatility of equipment for economy.
5 Complete chart.
6 Write a paragraph explaining which piece of whisking equipment produced the best cake, giving suitable reasons for your comments.

▶ ## FOLLOW UP

1 Have a short class discussion to discover whether any particular piece of equipment was more popular than the others, and also if there was any other piece which was especially disliked.

Compare the reasons for choice given in the charts to find out whether anyone produced any really different reasons from the rest of the class.

2   Taking into account the results presented in your own chart and in the discussion, suggest which of the pieces of equipment would be most suitable for the following people:
    a a newly married couple,
    b an arthritic pensioner,
    c a student living in a bed-sit.
    Give sensible reasons for your choice.

TEACHER'S NOTES

This assignment can be done as a group exercise in which each piece of equipment is tested by one member.

The preparation should ideally take the form of a discussion in the first instance, when various types of equipment can be suggested according to availability.

Information in the practical room should be provided to discover the method, oven temperature, cooking time, as well as the price and possible alternative functions of the equipment.

The more astute pupil will quickly grasp the implications of having numerous pieces of equipment all doing only one job, while a more comprehensive article may serve more than one purpose and thus earn its keep.

Less able candidates may be able to pursue the evaluation process through various degrees and may require some assistance to complete the task adequately.

While the practical work is a group study, the introduction to the assignment could take the form of a demonstration in order to recap:
    a the method of cooking,
    b the finish,
    c presentation,
    d raising agents,
    e low fat diets.

It may be possible to reduce the demonstration to a 'spot dem.' in order to speed up the lesson.

ASSIGNMENT 2

Batter mixes can be used to make both sweet and savoury dishes relatively cheaply, and many people choose to make them from packet mixes.

Compare the results from a home-made batter and from a packet mixture so that you can write a full report for the consumer page in your school magazine.

▶ ## PREPARATION

1 Give basic recipe, method and oven temperature.
2 Discuss consistency.
3 Choose appropriate baking tins.
4 Formulate class discussion on expectations regarding Yorkshire Puddings, i.e. What do you think they should come out like?

▶ ## PRACTICAL

Step 1
Working in groups of 4, each choose a different flour from those on display and use it to prepare a basic Yorkshire Pudding mixture.
Evaluate the results of each mixture.

Step 2
Working in groups, and using the recipe which you consider produced the best pudding, compare it with a packet Yorkshire Pudding mixture.
Compare the finished results taking into consideration flavour, colour, texture, cost and cooking time.

Step 3
Class lesson with demonstration by teacher. Study other dishes using a batter base, e.g., pancakes, dropscones, fritters.

▶ ## FOLLOW UP

1 Collate individual and group results to produce a chart indicating the differences in various dishes.
2 Cost the finished products.
3 Examine listed contents of packet mix compared with home-made.
4 Discuss other possible uses of batters.
5 Write a comprehensive report on your findings as a consumer guide for readers of your magazine.

TEACHER'S NOTES

This is an exercise which can be used as follows:

   a recap lesson on types of flour,

   b part of series of lessons on raising agents,

   c introduction of different type of scone mixture,

   d introduction to coating batters for frying,

   e recap on deep fat frying,

   f recap on fats and oils and temperatures,

   g uses of various batters in meal planning.

The use of a demonstration to bring all of this information together reinforces the points previously made regarding basic skills, cooking techniques, kitchen hygiene, and safety in the kitchen.

This is a complex assignment which needs a great deal of forward planning for it to be successful. It may be spread over a number of lessons to accommodate the slower student, but with the more able the practical work might be completed in only 2 lessons with the follow-up work and the demonstration taking one more.

It is a topic which would ideally be used in 4th year by which time all of the topics which are listed above as 'recaps' should have been covered.

ASSIGNMENT 3

Protein coagulates with heat. Using three different types of heat, illustrate this statement with particular reference to eggs in the preparation of a simple breakfast for one person.

▶ **PREPARATION**

1 Discuss various methods of applying heat to eggs.

2 Look up different ways of cooking eggs and find appropriate recipes and methods to be used.

3 Devise various methods of assessing the degree of coagulation achieved and the length of time required.

4 Prepare evaluation chart.

▶ **PRACTICAL**

Working in groups of 3, each person chooses a different recipe and produces a breakfast main course with accompaniments and garnishes which can be eaten in class.

When ready each dish must be examined and assessed in accordance with the criteria worked out in preparation lesson.

▶ **FOLLOW UP**

The whole class should meet together to discuss the results. Whichever method of assessment has been chosen must be examined and all comments compiled into a list giving a complete picture of the results. List complete recipes for breakfast dishes chosen.

TEACHER'S NOTES

This assignment gives scope for a great deal of class discussion towards the decisions necessary regarding (a) the types of heat, and (b) the type of dishes chosen. With guidance the students should be able to produce such dishes as:

    a scrambled eggs,

    b poached eggs,

    c boiled eggs,

    d coddled eggs,

    e fried eggs.

Recipes and methods for these dishes must be available in the resource centre.

A further follow up to this lesson could take the form of a short demonstration in which selected members of the class can show their fellow students the effect of excessive or over-prolonged heat in each case. At this point reinforcement of frying and choice of equipment for egg-cooking could be brought in.

The nutritional value of eggs, methods of cooking and uses in cookery can be recapitulated at this point.

Students should finish this assignment with a comprehensive written study on egg cookery in the form of a project.

The amount and format of the information produced will vary considerably with the ability of the student.

More able pupils should show a greater in-depth scientific approach whilst those lower down in the range will be content with a superficial coverage of the topic.

ASSIGNMENT 4

Shortcrust pastry mixtures are widely available in packet form, frozen or freshly made. Using one of each of these products, together with an equivalent quantity of home-made mixture, prepare 4 batches of jam tarts.

▶ ## PREPARATION

1 Go on a class outing to the most convenient supermarkets and delicatessens in your area and choose the cheapest of the preparations above.

2 Make out a worksheet on which you record your prices.

3 Give recipe and method.

4 Give oven temperature.

5 Estimate number of tarts likely to be produced.

6 Prepare a chart listing the variations in preparation, cooking, taste, colour, texture, general appearance, cost.

▶ ## PRACTICAL

1 Work in groups of 4, each person preparing one of the above mentioned pastries.

2 Complete chart.

3 Have a class tasting session and prepare questionnaire regarding preference. *DO NOT* label the various pastries.

▶ ## FOLLOW UP

1 Collate questionnaires.

2 Class discussion on each product.

3 Cost of individual tarts in each case.

4 Situation in which each may be appropriate.

5 Ease of preparation for various members of community.

6 Other uses of shortcrust pastry.

TEACHER'S NOTES

This assignment can be tackled by pupils from years 1–5 and the depth of response will depend on both age and ability. It can be adapted to be very simple or as complex as opposite. For example, I would envisage 1st year pupils or less able students making 2 sets of tarts and making a very simple comparison, while older students would be able to produce in-depth reasoned comment regarding the investigation itself and the results.

Class discussion in the follow up should elicit opinion as well as facts regarding consumer work.

ASSIGNMENT 5

Some cuts of meat are better value for money than others. Using a lamb chop and a piece of stewing beef of equivalent weight, find out which would be a better buy for an elderly person on a limited income.

► ## PREPARATION

1 Investigate meat prices.

2 Find out which supplier has the cheapest meat.

3 Look up the nutritional value of meat.

4 Devise methods of comparison.

5 Choose methods of cooking the meat and suggest additions to make each into a meal for one person.

► ## PRACTICAL

1 Prepare the meat according to the agreed methods.

2 Weigh each piece of meat and assess waste.

3 Cook meat and serve with appropriate accompaniments and garnishes.

4 Draw up chart indicating relevant points in preparation and finished results.

► ## FOLLOW UP

Write a short paragraph to point out which piece of meat in your opinion provides the best value for money in this situation. Give realistic reasons for your choice.

TEACHER'S NOTES

In this assignment students should become aware of the amount of inedible waste on certain cuts of meat. This is to include fat, bone and gristle.

The weight of the meat before and after preparation and cooking should be considered and this may be an area in which the pupils will need some guidance.

The appropriate choice of accompaniments and garnishes will bring out the more aesthetically aware candidates and will indicate the assimilation of nutrition in previous lessons. An unimaginative choice of sauces, vegetables and garnishes may be expected from less able students, while the more thoughtful pupil may well be able to make an attractive presentation even after the meat has been almost dissected. The correct amount of vegetables, etc., will also be difficult for children who are more accustomed to cooking for more than one person.

Recap on cuts of meat.

Recap on methods of cooking used.

Suggestions for alternative methods of cooking and presentation.

It would be a good idea to discuss meat prices generally so that students can be aware that not all meat is of the same quality and therefore the cheapest is not necessarily the best and one needs to shop around in order to get the best possible value for money.

ASSIGNMENT 6

Many people find difficulty in preparing fruit and vegetables without wasting quite a large percentage of food in the peel.

Using a paring knife and a swivel blade peeler, compare the amount of waste from:

    a one carrot, and
    b one eating apple.

Using the prepared ingredients, plus some cabbage, onion and mayonnaise, make a bowl of coleslaw.

► PREPARATION

1 Give recipe and method for coleslaw.
2 Arrange to work in pairs so that both carrots and apples will be used up. One person will use a knife on both items and the other a peeler. The peelings must be kept carefully so that they can be weighed.
3 Compare appearance of various peelers and vegetable knives.
4 Work out pie chart to indicate amount of waste in each instance.

► PRACTICAL

1 Weigh carrots.
2 Peel in non-overlapping strips from stem to root, removing as little as possible.
3 Cut off tops and roots sparingly.
4 Weigh peeled carrot and record waste.
5 Record weight of waste peel and tops.
6 Repeat with apples.
7 Prepare coleslaw.

► FOLLOW UP

1 Assemble charts for whole class.
2 Work out percentage of waste on carrots.
3 Work out actual cost of carrots and apples after preparation.
4 Make a pie chart for whole class for apples and another for carrots.
5 Consider other methods of removing peel in the absence of peelers or knives, i.e., grating.
6 Work out nutritional value of coleslaw using food charts.

TEACHER'S NOTES

This is a good exercise in manipulation.

With dextrous candidates it will be completed quickly while the less able will be fairly slow.

Kitchen hygiene and correct vegetable preparation can be recapped together with correct cooking methods.

Vegetable composition and food value can be emphasised at this point.

ASSIGNMENT 7

You are working for a Guide/Scout badge in housekeeping and need to display your knowledge of sensible shopping.

Compare the contents of 4 different brands of tinned carrots and make a chart showing the relevant information. Also, make a pie diagram indicating the percentage of carrots and liquid per can using the following formula:

$$\text{Percentage of solids} = \frac{\text{Weight of carrots}}{\text{Weight of carrots plus liquid}} \times 100$$

▶ PREPARATION

1 Check various brands of tinned carrots.

2 Purchase 4 cans of equal weight and content.

3 Discuss format of charts.

▶ PRACTICAL

1 Find total weight of each can.

2 Open can, empty out contents and weigh empty can.

3 Weigh the carrots after straining off liquid.

4 Make chart, filling in required details.

▶ FOLLOW UP

1 Discover which can contains the highest percentage of carrots.

2 Work out how much the carrots cost per pound.

3 Check the cost of canned carrots against the price of fresh carrots.

4 Discuss ways in which the liquid may be used to minimise waste.

5 Read label information carefully and compare contents.

6 Discuss the danger to health of having salt added to canned foods.

7 Reach a conclusion as to which is the best value for money. Is the most expensive the best?

8 Suggest situations in which canned vegetables can be useful.

9 Find out the nutritional value of tinned carrots.

TEACHER'S NOTES

This assignment can be used on more than one occasion by changing the type of food used.

As it stands it is very simple and the less astute pupil will probably take it at its face value and offer little or no extra information. Brighter pupils can be stretched by being guided to compare the contents information on the label and also to check the vitamin C content in the solids and water. This latter part could form part of another practical follow up lesson.

There can be a number of spin-offs from this investigation, e.g.,

      a preservatives—as found on labels,
      b food colourings added to carrots,
      c type of liquid used,
      d amount of liquid used,
      e comparative costs,
      f appearance of the carrots.

This assignment could be linked with Assignment 6 where the preparation of carrots is discussed. The time-saving factor of using cans as opposed to fresh vegetables should be brought in.

ASSIGNMENT 8

A pressure cooker is a valuable piece of equipment for busy people. Using a conventional steam pan and a pressure cooker, prepare a steamed pudding from a creamed mixture.

In addition, prepare, cook and serve an appropriate starter and main course to make a three-course meal for 2 people. Work in pairs.

► PREPARATION

1 Look up recipe for creaming method.

2 Choose extra dishes for meal.

3 Work out recipes to cook for 2.

4 Make schedule for whole meal.

5 Find out theory of steaming and pressure cooking.

► PRACTICAL

1 Make up one batch of a creamed pudding mix to be divided equally for comparison.

2 Prepare, cook and serve whole meal indicating correct accompaniments and garnishes.

3 Make notes on finished puddings, including times for preparation and cooking, as well as finished appearance and taste.

4 Where timing is appropriate, the meal may be eaten in class.

► FOLLOW UP

Prepare chart to illustrate findings. Discuss choice of extra dishes. Suggest various ways in which a pressure cooker can be of assistance in the preparation of meals.

Investigate the different types of pressure cookers available.

TEACHER'S NOTES

Theory of steaming and pressure cooking can be introduced. This would include the preparation of the container in which the pudding would be cooked.

Explain different methods of steaming, i.e. between 2 plates over boiling water, or on a trivet in a pan of boiling water. Suggest which foods would be suitable for each method.

It is sensible here to bring in the nutritional value of steamed foods plus the fact that they are generally recognised as being more easily digested, particularly in the case of fish or poultry for invalids. A useful point to mention would be the absence of fat in the cooking of these foods.

Less dextrous students find the removal of skin from fish much easier after steaming and there is less chance of wasting the fish which can cling to raw skin.

Caravanners find pressure cookers invaluable in the preparation of entire meals within one saucepan with the minimum of gas used.

Fuel economy in the use of the top of the cooker can be discussed.

Time saving on a variety of dishes.

Recaps steaming method.

Differences in appearances and taste.

Suggestion regarding preparation of complete meals in the pressure cooker.

Discussion of which members of the community would be most likely to benefit from a pressure cooker.

Mention of cheaper cuts of meat being tenderised in the pressure cooker and then finished off under the grill to give a more attractive appearance.

ASSIGNMENT 9

Mince is one of the cheapest meats but it can be very versatile. Collect a number of recipes for dishes in which mince is used. Prepare one of these dishes and serve it as part of a two-course lunch for you and your parents.

▶ ## PREPARATION

1   Find out the various types of mince available and their prices.

2   List as many different recipes as possible.

3   Work out the menu for your lunch.

4   Cost your whole lunch.

5   Work out the nutritional value of your meal.

6   Make out a shopping list and work schedule.

▶ ## PRACTICAL

1   Prepare, cook and serve the meal.

2   Work out the actual preparation time compared with the estimate on your time plan.

▶ ## FOLLOW UP

Discuss the various meals produced. Compare prices of the different dishes. Note how much the accompaniments added to the price of the meal (it is not really economical to use cheap meat and then spend a lot of money on out of season vegetables).

TEACHER'S NOTES

The comparison between minced beef, minced steak and beef mince could be interesting since the prices are very different from shop to shop. It may be advantageous to note the amount of fat in each type. The scientific lesson of actually weighing and comparing the various types of mince for cost and fat content would provide a further follow up session.

International dishes, such as chilli con carne, curry and spaghetti bolognese and lasagne, are useful for this type of assignment since they make a little meat go a long way and also bring in other methods of cooking, e.g., roux sauces and pasta cookery, together with herbs and spices. A useful exercise would be to have an Italian or Mexican party for the end of term when traditional accompaniments can be brought in.

Skills shown, e.g., menu planning, costing, nutritional analysis, economy of time and money, meat cookery, veg cookery, interesting presentation.

For the purpose of pupil assessment, the teacher could make a chart for the entire group using the above headings as guidelines. Marks for each process being listed against each pupil according to preparation, practical and follow up approaches and results. The amount of guidance required and given must be taken into consideration and marks deducted accordingly. In this way, the more imaginative and capable pupils will be marked solely on their own merit, while the less able will have lower results in accordance with the amount of assistance required.

In areas where they are readily available, beef may be replaced by lamb or pork, and these variations would lead to a very different group of recipes being used. It may be of value to repeat the assignment using different types of meat and then the student recipe file would benefit.

Many international recipes call for very interesting cooking and serving dishes which make for impressive presentation which would really make an impact at the end of term party.

ASSIGNMENT 10

You are working on a project on white fish in your Science lesson and as part of this work you need to prepare and cook some haddock. Your Science teacher and two friends are to join you in eating the dish you prepare as part of your assessment.

1 Purchase two haddock fillets and a whole haddock of equal weight.

2 Remove head and bones from whole haddock and divide into two fillets.

3 Remove skin from all fillets.

4 Prepare, cook and serve a simple main course for four people using the fish fillets and suitable accompaniments and garnishes.

▶ ## PREPARATION

1 Cost whole fish and also fillets and compare with equal weight of fish fingers.
2 Find out food value of white fish.
3 Look for recipes using white fish.
4 Plan the required meal.
5 Notes on classification of fish.
6 Lesson on filleting fish.

▶ ## PRACTICAL

1 Prepare fish as set in assignment.
2 Weigh waste from whole fish.
3 Weigh waste from fillets.
4 Make chart showing each weight.
5 Weigh remaining fillets.
6 Cost fillets.
7 Prepare meal.

▶ ## FOLLOW UP

1 Complete chart showing which of the pairs of fillets is best value for money.
2 Work out food value of complete dish.
3 Discuss occasions when this meal will be appropriate.
4 Suggest variations on recipe to make the meal suitable for various members of the family.

TEACHER'S NOTES

This assignment can be repeated using (a) oily fish, or (b) shellfish.

Methods of cooking fish can be introduced.

Réchauffé cookery recapitulated or introduced.

Sauce cookery recapped.

Vegetable preparation recapped.

Methods of cookery, i.e., steaming, recapped.

Invalid and infant cookery as well as cookery for special diets, i.e., low fat would be very appropriate here.

Dexterity of pupils will be tested in this assignment since it is not always easy to remove bones economically. Accurate weighing at all stages is important.

If the preparation lesson is done in great enough detail, the more able pupil will be able to consider the use of bones and skin in making stock for the sauce.

Regional cookery can be discussed at this point.

Because this is a meal which is to be assessed it must be attractively displayed so a selection of suitable serving dishes should be made available.

Colourful and appetising accompaniments and garnishes are essential since they play such a large part in making fish appealing to those who tend to stick to the fish and chip shop for their supplies of fish.

Geographical and environmental aspects of the drop in the quantities of fish available in the world today, together with the historical side of the fishing industry going right back to the Bible can add a great deal of interest to this topic. This will link up with work done in other departments of the school and could make an excellent base for an open evening display.

ASSIGNMENT 11

We are being made more and more aware of the dangers of using too many animal fats in our diet. As a result, manufacturers are putting more and more different types of fat on the market.

Choose 4 different soft margarines or low fat spreads and use them to prepare a basic Victoria sandwich cake in order to discover which you could recommend to a family that likes cakes but is trying to reduce its animal fat intake.

► PREPARATION

1 Visit the local supermarket and look at the various tubs of margarine on display to find out which are suitable for baking.
2 Check the prices of each type.
3 Working in groups of 4, each individual chooses a different tub of margarine to make his/her cake.
4 Find recipe for Victoria sandwich cake and list ingredients.

► PRACTICAL

Working individually within the group situation, each person prepares a basic mixture, using the chosen fats or spreads to produce a simple sandwich cake.

At the end of the lesson, each pupil should be able to produce a well-documented chart indicating:

   a preparation time,
   b ease of creaming,
   c cooking time,
   d cost of cake,
   e finished appearance,
   f prepared questionnaire to be completed by those eating the cake,
   g finished weight of cake.

► FOLLOW UP

1 Class discussion on finished result.
2 Questionnaire results.
3 Suggestions for variations on recipe, i.e., flavours.
4 Use of creaming method for other dishes, i.e., steamed puddings and rich cake mixtures.
5 Comparison of finished weights. Loss of moisture in cooking will be indicated here.

TEACHER'S NOTES

This assignment can be used very early in the course so that lower school pupils can be made aware of the various fats available. It would also be useful to discuss the vitamins A and D which are added to margarines.

A comparison of the various methods of packaging and the reasons for each type could be useful here.

A demonstration lesson on creaming method would be of value. The preparation and lining of a sandwich cake tin is important at this point.

Various shapings of cakes made by the creaming method can be introduced.

If used later in the course, a further follow up lesson on decoration can be brought in.

This is a good assignment in which to introduce or reinforce the NACNE recommendations on fats and health.

ASSIGNMENT 12

Too much sugar is now considered to be harmful to the body as a whole as well as to the teeth. However, many people still enjoy eating sweet-tasting foods and don't want to give them up entirely. Prepare, cook and serve 2 cakes using a creaming method, using a traditional method for one and some other form of sweetening agent for the second. Serve them to the class and evaluate the results in chart form.

▶ PREPARATION

1 Sources of sugar.

2 Stages in the production and refinement of sugar.

3 Food value of sugar.

4 Diseases caused by excess sugar.

5 Various methods of alternative natural sweetening, e.g., sultanas, dates, currants, raisins, banana.

6 Cake recipe using sugar.

7 Cake recipe using other form of sweetener.

8 Draw up chart showing contents, cost and variations on recipe.

▶ PRACTICAL

1 Prepare and cook cakes.

2 Complete chart up to tasting session.

3 Class evaluation.

4 Finish chart.

▶ FOLLOW UP

1 Class discussion on results.

2 Cost of original and alternative cakes.

3 Food value of each.

4 Discussion of further alternative sweeteners.

5 Appearance, texture and keeping qualities.

TEACHER'S NOTES

In this assignment a moderate amount of guidance will be required, since substitution of other foods for sugar is comparatively new and may not be familiar to students.

A recap of creaming method can be used.

Mention of various types of sugar plus their production and the processes involved.

Use of honey and syrup can be mentioned, together with dried fruits and banana.

Special diets requiring sugar-free meals, i.e., diabetics, should be brought in at this point.

Slimming meals could be a further follow up to this.

ASSIGNMENT 13

Bread mixtures are very simple to make and home-baked bread is very appealing.

Prepare and cook a basic 200 g bread dough, following the instructions on a packet of quick-acting yeast. Make up a second batch of dough, altering the method in any way you wish in order to try to make the bread come out wrong.

▶ PREPARATION

Work in pairs: one person make up a dough using the correct method and one choose an incorrect alternative. These alternatives will depend upon the theory of yeast being studied in advance, so that students are aware of conditions normally required for the production of acceptable yeast mixtures. Recipes and methods should be formulated at this point.

▶ PRACTICAL

Prepare, cook and display a loaf of bread made by the method suggested on the yeast packet and another made using a deliberately incorrect variation on the recipe.

Make a chart to illustrate the differences.

Run a tasting and examination session with the entire class and note comments.

▶ FOLLOW UP

Collate information from charts on to one large class chart, including observations regarding taste, texture, rising and cooking time.

TEACHER'S NOTES

This investigation into the effect of adverse conditions on yeast can be an individual part of a larger yeast assignment, including a more scientific approach involving test tube work on the effects of heat, cold, excessive amounts of salt and sugar.

Theory of flour can be recapped—types, composition.

Theory of raising agents recapped.

Mention of sweet and savoury dishes using yeast base.

Shaping of bread and rolls should be reinforced or introduced.

ASSIGNMENT 14

A well made sauce can turn a plain dish into an exciting part of a meal. Prepare, cook and serve a three-course celebration meal which includes a roux sauce.

► ## PREPARATION

1 Choose dishes and appropriate accompaniments and garnishes.

2 List recipes and basic method and equipment.

3 Variations of basic roux sauce.

4 Prepare time plan.

5 Class discussion on sweet and savoury sauces.

► ## PRACTICAL

Prepare meal and serve in appropriate manner for the chosen occasion, e.g., birthday, anniversary.

Class to eat the meal in school.

► ## FOLLOW UP

This can be used as an end of term celebration when pupils invite a guest and entertain them as part of the course. The guest should then be requested to comment on the meal, the presentation, colour, texture and suitability for the occasion.

TEACHER'S NOTES

This assignment can be a valuable way of linking up with community studies on a similar type of lesson where guests from out of school can be invited to take part in the meal.

The less able pupil will copy the recipe given in preparation time verbatim. Guidance must be given here to prevent the production of numerous similar dishes. Suggestions for a number of dishes and adaptations of basic recipes will be needed.

Colour, texture, thickness, uses of sauces as binding agents or for cooking can be brought in at this point. More advanced candidates may be interested in using a chaudfroid sauce or a panada in their project but may be unaware of the relationships between these and roux sauces.

Many pupils relate roux sauce only to cheese or parsley sauces and the others, such as bechamel, espagnole, hot hollandaise, are unknown. These can widen the scope for more talented students and, at the same time, help give some inspiration to the less adventurous. This assignment can be the catalyst to spark off a number of meal-planning projects involving sauce cookery and also seasonal cookery, e.g., rum sauce with Christmas pudding, parsley sauce with fish, panada for croquettes using up leftovers.

Although this has been set out as a full meal assignment, where time is limited, it can be shortened to the preparation of only a main course dish which may be taken home. In this case students can be asked to suggest suitable starters and puddings to complement the chosen dish and also occasions for which it would be appropriate.

ASSIGNMENT 15

Soya beans are a valuable source of protein. Ways have now been found to make soya beans look and taste like meat. This product is called Textured Vegetable Protein (TVP).

Prepare, cook and serve:

　　a beefburgers using fresh mince,

　　b beefburgers using half fresh meat and half TVP,

　　c beefburgers using all TVP.

Add accompaniments and garnishes to make a simple supper dish.

► PREPARATION

1　Check price of fresh mince.
2　Check price of TVP.
3　Find out how much TVP is required to produce 50 g.
4　Compile recipes for beefburgers.

► PRACTICAL

Work in groups of 3, each person working with one product. Produce, cook and serve the beefburgers. Make a chart indicating cost, ease of mixing, preparation time for each type. Serve samples of the beefburgers in class and the remainder may be taken home.

► FOLLOW UP

1　Evaluate the appearance, taste and bulk of each meal.
2　Discuss the value of TVP in various diets.

TEACHER'S NOTES

This lesson can provide a valuable lead on to:

    a vegetarian diets,

    b food in the Third World,

    c low fat diets,

    d school meals,

    e low cost protein meals,

    f food storage.

Each of the above suggestions can be used as an individual assignment or as a medium for class discussion.

It can be of value for students wishing to follow courses in dietetics and institutional catering.

Other school subjects such as Geography, Biology and Maths can be brought into this topic making it of true cross-curricular value.

ASSIGNMENT 16

People living alone sometimes risk making themselves ill because they don't bother to prepare proper meals for themselves.

Plan a three-course meal for one person, taking into account the cost and the nutritive value and then cook it.

▶ ## PREPARATION

1 Decide which people are most likely to fit into the above category and choose one group for whom to cook.

2 Choose the menu, taking care to consider dietary requirements of the person for whom you are preparing the dish.

3 Scale down the quantities to cook for one person.

▶ ## PRACTICAL

1 Prepare, cook and serve the meal, making sure that the presentation is appropriate for the person being served.

2 Eat the meal in class.

3 Cost the meal and work out preparation time.

▶ ## FOLLOW UP

1 Class discussion on each individual assignment.

2 There should be a great diversity of choice so there will be a number of dishes to compare.

3 Compare cost of each meal.

TEACHER'S NOTES

This topic should elicit a wide variety of dishes, since the needs of the various members of the community who would be likely to fit into the single person category are extremely different.

Discussion should bring out:

    a pensioners,

    b widows/widowers,

    c students.

Each of these categories will bring out its own individual needs, ranging from teenage to elderly, including men and women of all ages.

Careful choice of correct nutrients for each one, combined with costings to suit all purses, should lead to an extremely interesting display of meals.

It would be interesting to prepare a set of tables showing foods suitable for each of the people for whom meals were prepared so that a diet plan for single persons would evolve. Some of these meals could be tried out by inviting people from each of the categories to dine with pupils and comment later on the foods they were given.

A small handbook could be produced at the end of the project and perhaps sold cheaply in aid of school funds.

There are several excellent recipe books on the market giving advice on the preparation of single portions.

ASSIGNMENT 17

Mashed potato is a common vegetable in Britain today and yet it can be served very badly indeed. Conduct a survey in school to discover which preparation of home-cooked mashed potato appeals to most of your school chums.

► ## PREPARATION

1 Devise various methods of cooking and presenting the potato.
2 Draw up a chart to indicate:
   a preparation time,   **e** colour,
   b cooking time,   **f** texture,
   c presentation time,   **g** taste.
   d cost,
3 Check prices of different types of potato.
4 Find out which types of potato are most suitable for mashing.
5 Devise various methods of mashing the cooked potato.

► ## PRACTICAL

1 Prepare and cook the potato to the point of mashing it.
2 Divide the potato equally according to the number of methods of mashing to be used.
3 Mash each according to the choice of utensil, adding the same quantity of chosen ingredients to each batch.
4 Serve finished product to pupils in class and note their reaction and comments on the previously prepared chart.

► ## FOLLOW UP

1 Complete the chart to give an overall summary of the investigation.
2 Suggest, with sensible reasons, situations in which each of the chosen methods would be appropriate. Use the information collated during the assignment to support your conclusions. Also take into consideration the members of the community who would be most likely to choose the methods used.

TEACHER'S NOTES

This is a very simple assignment which can bring out a number of interesting points and which can lead to a lively class discussion, provided that the preparation and the follow up are correctly monitored and channelled by the teacher.

It will be necessary to consider a number of alternative ways of mashing vegetables and it may be necessary to demonstrate the more unfamiliar, such as use of a food processor.

Most students will be *au fait* with the standard potato masher and also a fork, but few may consider the use of a sieve or even a rolling pin used in the style of a pestle and mortar. Each of these produces potato of a different texture and requires a varying length of time to accomplish an acceptable result.

Additions, such as salt, pepper, butter, milk, margarine, nutmeg or parsley, will also have a bearing on the palatability of the finished product but these may need to be suggested by the teacher in a class of less adventurous students.

The completed chart of the less able pupil will be less comprehensive than that of a candidate who has been capable of a more thoughtful approach to the variation and additives.

Having each pupil preparing the potato in more than one way will ensure that a number of skills will be displayed; for example:

    a vegetable preparation which avoids waste of time and product,
    b correct cooking of potato to produce a product which retains its shape, flavour and colour and, at the same time, is thoroughly cooked,
    c ergonomics in the correct use of utensils,
    d organisation and method in planning operation,
    e sensitivity in appreciation of flavour and texture of finished product,
    f ability to collate facts and comments accurately to produce an intelligent summary.

The final requirement of the follow up section of the assignment should bring out a factual summary of the various results, leading to a logical conclusion regarding areas where each method chosen would be most sensibly employed; for example, it would hardly be realistic to expect to use a food processor while on a camping holiday, nor would it make sense to look for substitutes if the correct equipment was to hand. Cost, time and ease of use and cleaning are all factors that should be considered in this essay.

Although this particular assignment deals solely with potato, it is possible to adapt it to suit other vegetables if further reinforcement of vegetable preparation is needed.

It can also be used as part of a lesson on accompaniments and garnishes.

Although the assignment is initially aimed at the mechanics and aesthetics of potato preparation, it would be sensible at this stage to reinforce the importance of this vegetable in the diet.

The Potato Marketing Board produces a great deal of information on varieties of potato together with charts showing which suit particular cooking processes. An examination of these together with some actual potato samples should prove an interesting eye opener for those who do not know that different varieties exist.

This lesson can be an excellent link with Humanities in the study of food problems throughout the world.

ASSIGNMENT 18

Prepare, cook and serve an attractively garnished breakfast dish of scrambled eggs for two people using a microwave oven. Repeat this process using a saucepan on a hob. Prepare a written report explaining which of the methods you found to be the better, taking into consideration the preparation time and the finished result. Serve the meal to members of your class.

▶ PREPARATION

1 Pupils must find out how to operate the microwave oven safely and correctly.
2 The recipe for scrambled eggs must be looked up—quantities, etc.
3 Cooking utensils to be chosen for each method.
4 Format of report must be discussed and decided.
5 Discuss correct serving of eggs.
6 Theory of egg nutrition.

▶ PRACTICAL

1 Prepare eggs by microwave method, timing each process accurately.
2 Prepare scrambled eggs in saucepan, again timing the process carefully.
3 Serve the dishes attractively.
4 Write up results.
5 Serve the meals to other members of the class.
6 Cost meal.

▶ FOLLOW UP

Discuss the results of the two methods of cooking. Collect comments from the class on texture, flavour, colour, etc.

TEACHER'S NOTES

This is a good lesson for the introduction of microwave cookery, since students will all be aware of the anticipated results. In some other forms of microwave cookery pupils may experience difficulty in accepting colourless results, whereas eggs are not expected to change colour.

The parts of the dish which cook most rapidly are very obvious and the retention of heat after cooking is displayed very graphically, i.e., the protein continues to harden.

Timing of this operation is of the utmost importance, since most of the TV advertising is done using only one egg which cooks extremely quickly. The multiplication of ingredients for more people increases the cooking time considerably and this is a very important aspect of microwave cookery. The time required to clean utensils after use should be noted since this is one of the more onerous aspects of scrambled egg preparation.

It will be interesting to see how many pupils cook the eggs to the point of separation when they end up with egg solids and fluid instead of an amalgamated mixture. Presentation is important in this assignment since scrambled eggs can be quite uninteresting unless garnished attractively.

The use of scrambled eggs in invalid and snack cookery as well as breakfast cookery can be discussed here. Other methods of egg cookery for various occasions would be appropriate at this point, since this can be the starting point for a series of assignments including the uses and properties of eggs in cookery.

This assignment should bring out the fact that microwave ovens are not necessarily quicker than conventional cookers in specific situations. Time taken during the cooking time to stir the mixture must be noted.

Theory of egg nutrition, the need for a good meal to begin the day, and the use of eggs for different meals should be discussed. The uses and properties of eggs in cookery can be the base for a subsequent demonstration lesson showing binding, coating, thickening and enriching. If used early in the course, it would be useful to demonstrate methods of determining freshness of eggs and also to examine the markings on egg cartons.

The need to prepare toast while the egg is being cooked may provide a problem for those who are unable to concentrate on more than one task at a time.

Some pupils may even leave the toast until the eggs are ready, in which case the eggs will continue to cook in their own heat making them overdone. Others may prepare the toast first and leave it to get cold. Both of these methods must lead to penalty points being taken off. The very well organised student will be capable of producing the eggs and toast simultaneously.

ASSIGNMENT 19

Melting chocolate can be very difficult to do correctly and if it becomes overheated it can become thick and granular. Choose 3 different methods of melting chocolate and use the chocolate to prepare mousse for a party dessert.

▶ ## PREPARATION

1 Find out how many different methods there are of melting chocolate.

2 Look up the recipe for chocolate mousse.

3 Cost the ingredients of the mousse.

4 Work out how many portions can be prepared from 50 g chocolate.

5 Consider how an ordinary mousse can be turned into a festive pudding.

▶ ## PRACTICAL

1 Work in groups of 3.

2 Prepare the separate mousses.

3 Serve in individually measured portions to members of the group. Take the remaining portion home.

4 Hold a competition to decide which is most festive when finished.

▶ ## FOLLOW UP

1 Discuss the various mousses with the "tasters".

2 Discuss comments made by family.

3 Decide which is the preferred method.

4 Award prize for competition.

TEACHER'S NOTES

Food value of chocolate, including iron content, can be discussed here. Also, the dangers of eating too much chocolate, i.e., sugar related diseases. Uses of chocolate in the production of cakes, puddings and sweets.

The calorific value of chocolate and the value of chocolate as an emergency snack when unable to obtain proper meals, e.g., climbers, people trapped in snow storms, etc.

A demonstration of making various shapes in chocolate can be incorporated into this lesson and the more able pupil may opt to make individual chocolate cups in which to serve the mousse. Easter eggs could be demonstrated at the appropriate time of year.

A subsequent lesson on chocolate cake decoration and possibly caraque work could be an end of term treat.

With a less able group these cakes could be decorated appropriately and used for a children's party in conjunction with the local playgroup.

ASSIGNMENT 20

Prepare, cook and serve two batches of shortcrust pastry, making one in the conventional way and the other using a food processor. Use these pastries to prepare some small savoury pies to sell at one of your school's evening activities.

▶ ## PREPARATION

1 Discuss the varied uses of shortcrust pastry and its current popularity because it uses less fat and can be made from Flora.

2 Look up the basic recipe and variations.

3 Work out quantities and recipes for the number of pies to be made.

4 Decide upon fillings.

5 Find out how the food processor works.

6 See if the recipe for pastry in the processor is the same as the basic hand-mixed pastry recipe.

▶ ## PRACTICAL

1 Prepare both lots of pastry, taking care to note time taken for each.

2 Make up and cook the pies.

3 Package the pies for sale.

4 Measure the amount of liquid used.

▶ ## FOLLOW UP

1 Compare the two recipes.

2 Compare the quantities of liquid used.

3 See which pastry was made more quickly.

4 Which pastry was easier to handle?

5 Discuss any changes which could be made to either pastry to improve the preparation or the finished result.

6 Cost the pies for the sale.

TEACHER'S NOTES

Pupils who have not used a processor before will need a demonstration lesson showing the correct attachments needed and the appropriate method of timing, e.g., will it be necessary to use the fastest speed or will the normal variable speed be suitable?

It will become evident that the amount of fat and/or liquid may need to be adjusted so that the pastry does not become too 'short'.

This can be a valuable exercise in batch-baking, and the multiplication of quantities necessary to produce more than one pie of a slightly smaller than normal size will probably tax even the more able pupil who might end up with pastry left over at the end of the lesson. A short spot demonstration on using up leftover pastry in a manner relevant to the lesson could be put in here very usefully, emphasising the need for economy.

A visit to the local baker's shop to check on the cost of similar pies would assist with the costing, and an investigation into the most suitable wrapping to show the pies to advantage without adding too much to the cost would be most helpful.

ASSIGNMENT 21

Cheese is a very useful commodity which can be used in many sweet and savoury dishes. Some cheeses are more suitable for cooking than others. Prepare three pizzas and choose a different type of cheese for each topping.

► ## PREPARATION

1 Look up the names of as many cheeses as you can in your local supermarket.

2 Find out where each one comes from.

3 See if any one is especially recommended for cooking.

4 Trace an outline map of the world and pinpoint where each cheese originates.

5 Find out the different types of milk used in the production of each cheese and the different processes in production.

6 Write out the recipe for pizza.

► ## PRACTICAL

Working in groups of 3 each person must prepare, cook and serve a pizza, using the same base and topping but choosing a different cheese.

Look at the three pizzas when they come out of the oven and are still hot. Cut each into quarters and taste some of each. Make a note of the colour and texture of each. Leave until cold and taste again—compare the differences.

► ## FOLLOW UP

1 Discuss the differences between the three types of cheese chosen.

2 Compare the texture of the cheeses when hot and cold.

3 Evaluate which of the cheeses used gave the most pleasing results.

4 Look at the origins of pizzas and the traditional cheese used to make them.

5 Talk about the place on the menu of pizza in Italy compared with Britain.

TEACHER'S NOTES

Pizza is a useful fast food in Britain nowadays but its place on the table of an Italian family is rather different. A very useful comparison can be made here between the type of 'starter' usually served in Britain and the traditional Italian pizza starter. This can lead into a lesson on meal-planning and the various occasions when pizza would be a suitable dish to serve.

The various kinds of cheese chosen will result in a vast difference in the results of the finished pizzas. The very large numbers of cheeses on sale could mean that no two pupils use the same type.

Tasting the pizzas when hot and cold should show that some cheeses are stringy while others do not go down at all during cooking, and that most of them tend to go rather solid when cold. The flavour of some cheeses may be too bland or too strong for this purpose.

There is enough work on cheese to occupy more than one assignment lesson and it may be necessary to introduce the topic in a previous lesson with some project work—perhaps an investigation into British cheeses and their cooking properties.

The nutritional value of cheese is essential at this point either as a recap or a new topic.

With many younger pupils a tasting session is an interesting exercise because many will reject a raw cheese which they find acceptable cooked. Mozzarella is a typical example of a cheese which tastes infinitely better cooked.

The origins of cheese and the various milks used, ranging from skimmed cow's milk to goat's and ewe's milk and the very different processes involved in their production, are most interesting particularly if films or videos can be used to reinforce the written work. If the school is within easy reach of a cheese producing area, e.g., Stilton, Wensleydale, Cheddar, then a visit could round off the topic very successfully.

ASSIGNMENT 22

Many families eat toast for breakfast or use toast as a base for some other food, e.g., poached eggs. Some people use a toaster while others use a grill, both quite successfully.

Prepare six slices of toast using an electric toaster for two, an electric grill for two and a gas grill for the remainder. Using two loaves, select one slice from each for each method of toasting then compare and evaluate results.

► PREPARATION

1 Look at the various sliced loaves in the supermarket or local shop and see how many are recommended for toasting.

2 Check the prices on the loaves.

3 Divide into groups of 3 and decide which of the methods each will use.

4 Devise a chart to write up your finished results.

5 Choose the headings for your evaluation.

► PRACTICAL

1 Choose the types of bread you think will be most suitable for toasting from the selection available on the table.

2 Prepare the toast, timing the preparation accurately including the time needed to heat up the grill.

3 Cut the toast and examine each slice carefully to see which produced the most pleasant looking and tasting results.

► FOLLOW UP

1 Discuss the various toasts and decide first of all which type of bread was best for toasting.

2 Consider the time taken for each process.

3 Work out the cost per slice using the overall cost of the loaf and dividing it by the number of slices.

TEACHER'S NOTES

At its simplest, this is a very simple assignment which can be used from 1st year upwards with only the end product and the cost to be taken into consideration. More advanced pupils should be able to pursue this subject in greater depth and consider the cost of the toaster versus the cost of using a grill which is already there. The thickness of the bread and the consequent brittleness of the toast should be noted and the more scientific could progress to the loss of moisture during toasting. The production of Dextrin and then charring of toast should be discussed.

In the discussion of grill versus toaster, the types of grill which can be used in sections and the toasters which cook four slices of bread should be examined so that relative costs can be noted.

Safety aspects of using a toaster instead of a grill should be discussed.

The cost of various types of toaster on the market and their different functions could be a homework exercise for all pupils from year one onwards.

More able and interested students may find it interesting to work out the actual cost of using each appliance for toasting but this will need a very dedicated Physics-based approach.

The nutritive value of bread can be recapped or introduced at this point and note made of the value of bread even in calorie reduced diets. The fibre value of wholemeal bread must be emphasised at this juncture since we are now always working with NACNE in mind.

Lower school pupils may find it interesting to weigh the bread and work out how many calories are obtained from their daily intake.

ASSIGNMENT 23

Egg custards are nourishing and easily digested and are, therefore, very useful for special diets. However, it is very easy to produce an unacceptable custard by incorrect cooking. Prepare two baked egg custards using two different methods and evaluate the results, taking into consideration the appearance and texture. Suggest occasions when this dish could be served.

► PREPARATION

1 Look up the recipe, method and cooking temperature for baked egg custard.

2 Choose two methods for the baking.

3 Find out which diets would benefit from the inclusion of egg custards.

4 Prepare time plan.

5 Do written work on serving suggestions and suitable occasions when they could be included in the menu.

► PRACTICAL

1 Prepare and cook the custards according to the chosen methods.

2 Check on cooking temperature and time.

3 Turn the custards onto plates for serving.

4 Cut each in half and examine the texture.

5 Taste each custard.

► FOLLOW UP

1 Compare the texture and solidity of each custard.

2 Compare the colours of the finished products.

3 Compare the cooking times.

4 Discuss which method was more successful and why.

5 Class discussion on serving suggestions.

TEACHER'S NOTES

This can be a very deceptive assignment, since many pupils will take it only at face value unless guided carefully.

The coagulation of protein in eggs is the most important element in the baking and therefore pupils must be conversant with the temperatures at which a baked custard will set without boiling and introducing bubbles into the mixture. The use of a *bain-marie* can be demonstrated at this point.

The ability to recognise the point when a custard is set right through without turning rubbery or separating out is essential if a truly digestible dish is to be produced.

The ease of digestion leads to the various members of the community who would be likely to benefit from baked custards in their diets, i.e., invalids, convalescents, infants; and also their place in ordinary menus.

Many pupils may not recognise the filling in quiches as egg custards, nor do they always appreciate the value of creme caramel as a very suitable examination dish. The high biological-value protein content of egg custard makes it a very appropriate pudding for lacto-vegetarians, while vegans who eat free-range eggs could eat this dish if prepared from soya milk.

The overall nutritive value of eggs and milk in this dish can be reinforced at this point.

A display of the type of dishes most suitable for baked custards could be useful, particularly if their oven proof qualities are emphasised in order to avoid accidents. The ability to bake a custard while using the oven for other dishes is a pointer towards fuel economy which should not be omitted. Similarly, an assignment requiring use of the oven alone would benefit from the inclusion of this dish.

Egg production, grading, packaging costs could be topics for homework and the more adventurous student may even venture into the realms of free-range eggs versus battery eggs.

ASSIGNMENT 24

Fried foods can be soggy and indigestible unless they are correctly prepared before cooking and then properly cooked. Using three small fillets of white fish and three different methods of coating, prepare a supper dish for you and your parents, or the people with whom you live. Add the appropriate accompaniments and garnishes to make the dish interesting and appealing.

► PREPARATION

Look up frying as a method of cooking and find out the types of coating recommended for white fish. Also, find out the correct oil or fat temperature for cooking fish.

Decide how the dish is to be served and plan your work time according to the needs of the accompaniments and garnishes, as well as the preparation and cooking of the fish.

Write an account of the reasons for coating fish before frying.

Work out the quantities of coating required for each fillet.

► PRACTICAL

Prepare, cook and serve the supper dish according to the wording of the assignment.

► FOLLOW UP

Discuss the three coating methods chosen and give reasons for your choice.

Consider the additional nutritive value given by the coatings. Work out the nutritive value of the complete dish.

Suggest alternative accompaniments and also occasions when this dish would be appropriate.

Look carefully at the nutritive content of the meal and state which type of diet would not benefit from the inclusion of this meal. Give valid reasons for your comments.

TEACHER'S NOTES

This is a very full assignment which can be used to reinforce work on fats and oils, fish cookery, frying as a method of cooking, coating foods for frying and the use of accompaniments or garnishes. Low fat diets must also be mentioned here.

The food value of fish and its use in menu-planning, both as a starter and a main course, are important since fish can be a vastly underrated commodity. This may stem from the unpleasant smell we associate with stale fish, so a visit to a fish market where the catch has just been landed may provide an interesting insight into the correct appearance and lack of smell in *fresh* fish.

If possible, a video or film or a visit to a fish-processing factory would be an excellent way of stirring up interest in fish, since most children will eat fish fingers without even associating them with the fresh product.

The safety aspect of frying must not be missed out of this lesson, since so many kitchen fires can be traced back to frying pans being left unattended. This could lead to a whole lesson on kitchen safety.

The use of electric deep fat pans, as well as the ordinary pan with a basket, could be compared during this test but a demonstration may be needed before pupils can be allowed to use these themselves.

This can lead to a fuller discussion on the environment, over-fishing and pollution leading to world shortages of popular varieties of fish.

ASSIGNMENT 25

Many people do not care to drink milk but will accept it if it is disguised in dishes which look attractive. Prepare, cook and serve three dishes in which milk is the major ingredient and which will be likely to appeal to non milk drinkers.

► PREPARATION

1   Select three recipes which are made from milk.

2   Prepare a time plan and a shopping list.

3   Suggest suitable accompaniments and garnishes for each dish.

► PRACTICAL

Prepare, cook and serve the chosen dishes.

► FOLLOW UP

Each pupil should be able to talk briefly to the rest of the class giving an outline of reasons for choice, and also suggestions for occasions when these particular dishes could be included in the menu.

A discussion of how the dishes could be made with the various types of milk available would be useful, e.g., low fat menus using skimmed milk.

TEACHER'S NOTES

Milk is a vast subject in its simplest form and it becomes even more complex when all the various types of milk available are included. Because of this, the topic could take up many weeks if all areas of milk, its production, food value and cookery are to be investigated. In order to avoid the boredom of a topic which continues too long, it would be wise at this point to stick to pasteurised whole milk and pasteurised skimmed milk for in-depth investigation. Pupils can then build up a file on milk beginning with these two, since they are possibly the most well known. Work on the many milk variations can be continued in the form of a project, with pupils finding out quite a lot of information for themselves for homework and with the experimental aspects being pursued in class.

There are a number of simple experiments which can be done without needing any equipment other than that found in the kitchen, e.g., heating equal quantities of whole and skimmed milk to boiling point and observing the changes which occur over a period of 48 hours. This is only one of many basic milk investigations which are possible without the use of a laboratory. The Milk Marketing Board is very good about helping with this type of work.

The food value of milk dishes and their comparatively low cost are both topics which should be discussed here since economy is of such importance.

For lower school pupils, the initial introduction to milk as a 'perfect' food for young mammals is to be recommended, particularly if accompanied by visits to a milk processing plant or a dairy farm. Seeing calves or lambs feeding from their mothers or from bottles can be an excellent reinforcement of the nutrition lessons on milk. It may be possible to liaise with a child development group when they are planning a lesson on breast feeding.

Milk processing into the different varieties we see now provides a very good 'tasting' lesson when pupils can compare commodities such as condensed, evaporated, long life, skimmed and sterilised milks.

A folder of milk recipes would be helpful for future reference, particularly if the food value of the milk used in each is noted. This would cut down on the time used in choosing recipes for assignment work at examination time, as well as giving the pupils interesting recipe books of their own chosen dishes.

ASSIGNMENT 26

Yoghurt is a very popular food with all age groups but it can be a very costly item in a large household. It is very easy to make at home if you have a thermos flask with a wide neck, or you can use an electric, home yoghurt-maker. Using both of these, prepare one pint of yoghurt in each and compare them with bought natural yoghurt.

▶ PREPARATION

1   Look in the textbooks and find out how to prepare yoghurt at home in a flask.

2   Read the instruction leaflet which accompanies the electric yoghurt-maker.

3   Write out the appropriate recipes and work plans.

4   Check on the price of bought natural unflavoured yoghurt.

▶ PRACTICAL

1   Follow the instructions for each method of yoghurt-making.

2   Leave the yoghurt to stand for the required length of time.

▶ FOLLOW UP

1   When the correct time has elapsed, pour nearly all the yoghurt from the flask and leave the remainder for a further 24 hours.

2   Do the same with the machine made yoghurt, leaving one pot still keeping warm.

3   Refrigerate all yoghurts except those still incubating.

4   *Next day* refrigerate the remaining yoghurts.

5   Taste all yoghurts and decide which tastes best.

6   Compare with bought yoghurt.

7   Cost all yoghurts.

8   Suggest methods of flavouring yoghurts.

TEACHER'S NOTES

Yoghurt is a very interesting and popular food for experiment. Merely leaving some to incubate for a further 24 hours produces a dramatic alteration in flavour as the acidity becomes more pronounced.

It is interesting to note how pupils react to natural yoghurt rather than the flavoured sweetened types which are more popular, and the amount of sugar needed to make it acceptable can be quite considerable. It can be quite a complex exercise to produce a flavoured yoghurt which does not become runny in the process.

The history of yoghurt and its considerable medicinal qualities can provide a very interesting lesson. The use of yoghurt in producing make-up and toilet preparations will surely bring out a lot of feedback from younger girls. A display of yoghurt-based products would be valuable.

Yoghurt is being used a lot in natural and wholefood cookery and it would be rather nice if pupils could produce some dishes using their own home-made yoghurt. A visit to a health food shop to investigate the products on sale there which contain yoghurt may produce some surprising results.

The nutritive value of yoghurt must be included and emphasised here, since many children do not regard it as a food. A comparison of the various types on sale with and without additives will show that a great many do not have artificial sweeteners for example, but they do have extra sugar. This point can be important for those on low carbohydrate diets.

Home-made yoghurts can look rather pale and unappetising when they have been flavoured, but this is not something which can be remedied very easily without resource to artificial colourings which we are taking such pains to avoid. Pupils may come up with some suggestions for flavourings with strong colours which look more appealing. Experiments with jams, jellies and pie-fillings, as well as fresh fruits, should produce some interesting flavours.

Comparison of the cost of the various yoghurts should give some surprising results.

The correct sterilisation of equipment must be emphasised.

ASSIGNMENT 27

Your friend is a good cook who follows the recipe and instructions to the letter. However you think that your shortcuts are just as good so you have challenged her to a competition making flaky pastry. She is to make it by the conventional method, leaving it to chill and rest before cooking but you are going to miss out these parts of the recipe.

Each prepare a batch of sausage rolls according to your own method and compare the results.

▶ PREPARATION

1 Write out the recipe and method for flaky pastry.

2 Write out the method for sausage rolls.

3 Find out why cooling and resting of pastry is recommended.

4 Prepare a time plan for each batch.

▶ PRACTICAL

1 Working in pairs each student prepares 1 batch of pastry according to the individual time plan.

2 Note time taken for each.

3 Make brief notes on the 'handling' of each pastry.

4 Bake sausage rolls.

5 Look for any differences in the two pastries.

6 See how much fat lies on the baking tray after cooking.

7 Check weight of sausage rolls after cooking.

▶ FOLLOW UP

1 Class discussion on the results.

2 Notes on the uses of flaky pastry in sweet and savoury dishes.

3 Conclusion on the value of cooling and resting.

4 Compare weights of sausage rolls and amount of fat lost from each.

5 Comment on time taken in preparing each batch.

TEACHER'S NOTES

Flaky pastry can be a difficult topic for pupils since they do not readily accept the need for cooling and resting. On the other hand, the amount of time saved may possibly override any deficiencies in the pastry in the eyes of a busy housewife.

The high fat content may be discussed here along with the types of fat used.

A comparison between puff, rough puff and flaky pastry might bring out the fact that rough puff is less fatty and easier to make but, of course, this will only apply if the pupils have already had experience of making or seeing these pastries made. A demonstration lesson for comparative purposes could be useful here. The cost of each of these pastries should be noted, as should the amount produced from a very small quantity of flour.

Ease of handling must be monitored very carefully since many pupils will use too much flour on the table if the pastry becomes difficult. A measured amount of flour for dredging may be the answer to this.

The high calorific value of flaky pastry should be noted when considering its place in the diet and reference to the COMA report would not be out of place. At all stages in the course, mention of fat-related ailments must be emphasised in an effort to educate pupils at an early age in habits of healthy eating.

ASSIGNMENT 28

Home-made mayonnaise can add a very pleasing flavour to a dish or a salad. Using the same basic recipe, prepare two batches of mayonnaise using a blender for one and making the other using a hand whisk.

Using this mayonnaise, prepare and serve two dishes which would be suitable for serving as starters for a celebration evening meal. Evaluate the results according to timing and effort, colour and texture. Show these results in the form of a simple chart.

▶ PREPARATION

1 Look up the recipe for mayonnaise.

2 Find out how the blender works.

3 Read the blender guide book to discover how mayonnaise is made.

4 Prepare the chart ready to write up the results.

5 Decide which dishes to prepare.

6 Plan a worksheet to cover the whole task.

7 Check on the cost of ready-made mayonnaise.

8 Cost the ingredients for home-made mayonnaise.

▶ PRACTICAL

Prepare both batches of mayonnaise, taking care to time each process carefully including the cleaning of the equipment. Measure the quantity of mayonnaise obtained. Prepare and serve the two dishes as attractively as possible.

▶ FOLLOW UP

Compare the time taken for both batches of mayonnaise. Measure the amounts obtained compared with the purchased type. Decide which is better value for money.

Compare the colour, flavour and texture of all three mixtures. Write a paragraph discussing the merits or otherwise of each method of preparation.

Consider, in view of your findings regarding time and effort, which members of the community would be most likely to benefit from either method.

TEACHER'S NOTES

This is an excellent opportunity to introduce a property of eggs which is not readily used by students in examinations. The theory of lecithin as an emulsifier can be discussed.

Many pupils may not be conversant with the preparation of mayonnaise since salad cream is currently more widely purchased. A display of the various types of mayonnaise (flavoured and plain) together with a selection of bottled salad creams should bring out a very lively lesson. A careful study of the various labels and types of packaging, e.g., tubes could be interesting.

Comparisons of ingredients among all the bottles will elicit a great variety of seasonings which in themselves could lead to a project on herbs and spices.

The many ways in which mayonnaise can be incorporated into dishes may well surprise those who only see it on the side of a salad dish.

The amount of time and effort taken to produce mayonnaise using a hand-whisk may well lead to the conclusion that a blender is best, but the time taken to set up and clean a blender could offset this. These are points which may need to be discussed before pupils embark on the written work concerning those likely to benefit from blenders.

At this point, mention could be made of the elderly and handicapped, who may find this type of equipment very easy and useful to operate, but almost impossible to maintain.

Safety measures and comparison of different types of blender would be a suitable addition to this project.

Nutritional value of mayonnaise and lowered fat alternatives cannot be omitted from this lesson. Perhaps this aspect may be noticed during the inspection of labels and packages as above. More astute pupils will be aware of the differences.

ASSIGNMENT 29

Blanching is a cooking term which covers more than one topic, although all are concerned with the use of boiling water.

1 Find out three food processes which involve blanching.
2 Prepare one food using each process.
3 Having blanched the foods, go on to complete the processes either by storing the food or by using it in a finished dish.

Write an account of each process giving reasons for the need to blanch and the finished appearance of foods when they have been blanched.

► **PREPARATION**

1 The first thing to do here is to discuss what is meant by blanching. What does the word mean in its literal sense?

2 Find out why foods need to be blanched.

3 Decide which foods are to be used.

4 Compile recipes for use with the blanched foods.

5 Prepare a time plan to cover the blanching and the dishes being prepared.

► **PRACTICAL**

Prepare, cook and serve or store the chosen dishes.

► **FOLLOW UP**

1 Complete written work on assignment.

2 Discuss the various reasons for blanching as they apply to each dish.

3 Consider the effect of freezing vegetables without blanching.

4 Investigate any other methods of blanching other than by boiling water.

TEACHER'S NOTES

Most pupils will be acquainted with the term 'blanching' in the context of home freezing but may not be so familiar with the method being used to remove skins from fruit, vegetables and nuts or, indeed, to reduce over-flavouring in some cured meats such as bacon joints.

They may need a considerable amount of guidance from the teacher in this since school textbooks tend to be rather vague in their approach to the topic.

The theory of freezing and the need to arrest the growth of organisms in foods to be frozen are very important at this point, and it would be a good idea to demonstrate the use of a blanching basket. The need to cool foods rapidly for freezing must be reinforced or the temperature in the freezer will rise unacceptably.

It would be a good idea to bring in at this point that it is not always desirable to remove skins from foods such as tomatoes, as this removes some of the dietary fibre. Freezer packaging must be included if any pupils opt for freezing as part of the assignment. A display of commercial packaging and also makeshift packages which can be found in the home would be useful since many people are put off freezing by the cost of recommended packaging.

If necessary, as with a low ability group, it may be a good idea to divide this assignment into three parts and deal with each aspect of blanching separately.

A further follow up assignment using the frozen food would reinforce the initial work done.

The dishes chosen by the pupils to incorporate blanched foods will vary according to the amount of guidance given in the preparation session.

ASSIGNMENT 30

When making a pastry fruit flan it is necessary to use a glaze in order to prevent the fruit from drying out and also to improve the appearance. Prepare three flans using tinned fruit and a different glazing agent on each.

▶ ## PREPARATION

1 Class divides into groups of 3.

2 Find out what glazes are available.

3 Decide which glaze each is going to use.

4 Look up recipe for flan.

5 Look up recipes for each type of glaze.

6 Prepare a work sheet on which can be noted the ease of preparation, the preparation time, appearance and the cost of each.

7 Find out the nutritional value of each.

8 Check any commercial glazes for additives.

▶ ## PRACTICAL

1 Prepare and cook the flans.

2 Complete the chart after comparing the appearance of the flans.

▶ ## FOLLOW UP

1 Work out the total cost of each flan.

2 Work out the nutritional value and see how much has been added to the flan by the glaze.

3 List occasions when this type of flan would be appropriate.

4 Consider ways of making the flan more attractive to look at for special occasions.

TEACHER'S NOTES

The use of different glazes can be quite confusing so this assignment can be of value in explaining the differences and the scientific principles behind each type. Reference to artificial colouring and flavouring will be appropriate, as will discussion on the amount of sugar added. If sugar free fruit is used for the flan, the amount of extra sugar obtained from commercially prepared glaze will alter the food value considerably. Mention of the importance of knowing the exact carbohydrate content for those on special diets.

This is also a useful exercise for the recap of baking a fluted flan ring, baking blind and also the preparation of rich flan pastry.

ASSIGNMENT 31

Apple pie is a very popular dessert but sometimes the fruit inside is not always as soft and palatable as it might be. Working in groups devise three different methods of preparing the fruit and, using one of these processes each, prepare and cook a pie which can be served as part of a Sunday lunch.

▶ PREPARATION

1 Get together in groups of 3 and discuss which method each is to use.

2 Look up the recipe and oven temperature for the pastry.

3 Check on the recommended cooking times for apple pies.

▶ PRACTICAL

1 Prepare and cook the pies according to the method chosen.

2 Time the preparation carefully.

3 Observe the colour of the fruit after preparation.

4 Check the cooking time, making sure that the apple is thoroughly cooked right through.

5 Compare the finished appearance of each of the pies with the others.

▶ FOLLOW UP

1 Compare the findings regarding the preparation and cooking times.

2 Look at any pies which contained raw apple and consider whether the pastry suffered overcooking in order to get the apple softened.

3 See if the cooked apple made the pastry soggy on the base because of the juices being released before the pastry is set.

TEACHER'S NOTES

Apple pies seem to be among the best foods for investigative cookery because they involve so many basic skills. This assignment brings together and reinforces:

a   the making of shortcrust pastry,

b   fruit preparation,

c   use of vegetable knife and peeler.

d   use of grater,

e   stewing,

f   lining and covering a pie plate,

g   correct 'finishing' of plate pies.

It will be necessary to discuss enzymic browning of fruit and ways to counteract this, otherwise the finished pies will be discoloured.

The length of time and the amount of cut surface exposed to air must be taken into account when looking at the browning of fruit. Some guidance may be necessary in the choice of methods of preparation.

In the case of the cooked fruit, it must be cooled adequately so that the heat doesn't spoil the pastry or even make it completely unmanageable.

This assignment could be used with lower school children as well as examination candidates in which case a full demonstration of shortcrust pastry, lining and covering a pie and preparing the fruit will be necessary.

A comparison of the appearance should show the way in which the fruit leaves a lumpy appearance in the pastry as it cooks to a soft consistency after the pastry has set. This may leave a gap between the top pastry and the fruit.

A display of bought fruit pies and a list of their contents should bring out a good deal of discussion on nutrition and cost of home-made pies.

ASSIGNMENT 32

Your Granny is very fond of home-baked bread but scorns the modern packet mixtures and what she calls 'new-fangled methods'. In order to show her how good quickly-made bread can be, prepare a loaf using a packet mix and also a loaf using the Chorleywood method. Use some of each of the finished loaves to make some sandwiches to take to her house for tea.

▶ ## PREPARATION

1 Look at the various packets of bread mix and bring the one which will give you sufficient quantity to make one loaf of bread.

2 Find out what is meant by the Chorleywood method.

3 Look up the correct recipe for a 1 lb loaf using this method.

4 Cost the two loaves.

5 Decide upon the sandwich fillings and packaging materials.

▶ ## PRACTICAL

1 Make up the two loaves of bread.

2 Make a careful note of the time taken to prepare each loaf.

3 Check the amount of liquid required by each method.

4 Take note of the time taken to prepare and also to mix.

5 Weigh the two loaves.

6 Prepare the sandwich filling and make the sandwiches. Pack them carefully.

▶ ## FOLLOW UP

1 Compare the cost in money and time of the two loaves.

2 Consider the size of each loaf in relation to the other.

3 Decide which loaf is better value for money.

4 Look at the packet to see what additives have been put in.

TEACHER'S NOTES

This will be a good opportunity to go over the various methods of bread-making and reference can be made to the original methods when baking bread took all day. A visit to a museum where old fashioned crafts are displayed would be interesting. A collection of old bread tins and modern ones could illustrate the advances made in household technology. Types of flour—strong plain—origins of flours. Origin of yeast and the production of dried yeast could be a different side step to those interested.

Discussion of why bread needs to be kneaded and why ascorbic acid is added must be included in this lesson. Oven temperatures, cooking time and the method of testing to determine when the bread is cooked are important. A further series of follow up lessons can be introduced to demonstrate the uses of sweet dough and various shapings of bread, both novelty and traditional. Baking loaves in plant pots could provide a little extra interest.

Consideration of the types of packaging used for commercial bread is important together with the information given on wrappers.

Suitable sandwich fillings and wrappings need to be discussed fully.

The types of flour used in bread-making and the areas in which the grains are grown are aspects of the topic which can be linked with Humanities and will bring in world food problems.

ASSIGNMENT 33

Green vegetables are a very important source of vitamins and minerals in our diet provided that they are correctly prepared and cooked. Using 400 g brussels sprouts, investigate 4 different ways of cooking in order to discover which will retain the maximum nutritional food value, flavour and eye appeal.

► PREPARATION

1 Find out the correct method of preparing and cooking brussels sprouts.

2 Discuss variations on the correct cooking method.

3 Consider why salt or sodium bicarbonate should or should not be added when cooking.

4 Investigate the vitamin loss in the preparation and cooking of vegetables.

5 Make an interim decision as to which will produce the best results in the light of above.

6 Make out a chart showing the times and methods, leaving a space for the results, i.e., colour, texture, firmness.

► PRACTICAL

Prepare and cook the sprouts according to the assignment.

► FOLLOW UP

1 Set out each set of sprouts for examination.

2 Cut one of each set so that the centre can be observed.

3 Look at each dish and discuss colour, texture and taste.

4 Fill in chart.

TEACHER'S NOTES

This is the shortest of these assignments and it can be completed in one practical lesson. However, the amount of theory which must precede and follow it can be considerable, since the vitamin content of the sprouts will be altered considerably by the methods of cooking used.

It would be a good time to go into the uses and absorption/loss of vitamin C in depth since it is one time when a vegetable like this will come under close scrutiny in the classroom.

Surprisingly, children rarely opt to use green vegetables as accompaniments when choosing assignment dishes and perhaps this is because they seldom encounter them properly and appetisingly cooked.

If possible, a visit to a science laboratory to determine the amount of vitamin C left in the sprouts after cooking would be a real bonus.

The connection between the storage, preparation and cooking and vitamin C loss must be emphasised and it would be appropriate to mention other green leafy vegetables in this context.

The use of liquid in which green vegetables have been cooked must be discussed here.

The following suggestions can be put forward if the students are not able to devise four methods for themselves.

a cook $\frac{1}{4}$ of them by putting them into one pint of cold water, bringing to the boil and cooking for 10 minutes,

b drop $\frac{1}{4}$ into one pint of rapidly boiling water and cook for 10 minutes,

c drop $\frac{1}{4}$ into one pint of rapidly boiling water and cook for 5 minutes,

d drop $\frac{1}{4}$ into one pint of rapidly boiling water containing one teaspoon bicarbonate of soda and cook for 5 minutes.

In each case use a saucepan with a close-fitting lid.

ASSIGNMENT 34

You have a new microwave oven and have been trying out a number of different recipes. The last one you tried was lemon curd which only needed egg yolks so you have some whites left over. Meringues are useful for using up egg whites because they can be stored in an airtight tin for a short time.

Make up a batch of meringue mixture and cook half in your new microwave and half in a conventional oven.

Observe the preparation and cooking time in each case.

▶ ## PREPARATION

1   Look up the recipe for meringues made by the conventional method.

2   Read the instructions for making meringues in a microwave oven.

3   Prepare a time plan.

▶ ## PRACTICAL

1   Make the meringues following each recipe accurately.

2   Write a short account describing the difference in the preparation and cooking of the two batches.

3   Set out results and compare colour, texture and general appearance.

▶ ## FOLLOW UP

1   Discuss the results of the practical lesson.

2   Decide how and when the meringues can be used.

TEACHER'S NOTES

Many pupils would like to make meringues in school but have little success because of the time involved. However, microwave cookery has altered this and very close textured crisp meringues can be produced in a very short time. The difference in the preparation is also very marked and the microwaved cakes are fascinating to watch during cooking.

This is a very pleasant assignment which can be used as a treat as well as an exercise.

The meringue shapes produced can be made into a pudding or cakes at a later date when cake decorating and decorative presentation could be the theme.

This would be a good moment to draw a comparison between the soft-centred meringue seen in lemon meringue pies and the crisp variety produced here. The time taken to prepare and cook and the very different textures must also be noted carefully.

An exercise of this kind would be most appropriate following a lesson on making lemon curd in a microwave oven where only the egg yolks are required. Alternatively, it would be useful to use up left over egg whites after making almond paste for simnel cakes. The meringues could then be made into suitable shapes to decorate the top of the cake.

Reinforcement of the way in which microwaves work is essential in this lesson since it really does illustrate very clearly how the water in the egg white is dried out, compared with that cooked in a conventional oven.

ASSIGNMENT 35

Your aunt has been ill and needs building up but she has little appetite for heavy meals. She is very fond of custard and you are planning to make some for her dessert on Sunday.

Prepare a pouring custard sauce with an egg base which can be served with some stewed fruit. In addition prepare some custard for your family using a packet mix.

Compare the nutritional value of the two custards.

▶ ## PREPARATION

1 Write out the recipe and method for each custard.
2 Find out about the use of a double boiler.
3 Find out why a double boiler is desirable in the preparation of egg custard.
4 Look up the theory of protein coagulation.

▶ ## PRACTICAL

1 Prepare both types of custard according to the recipe sheets.
2 Time both methods carefully.
3 Measure quantity obtained from each pint of milk used.
4 Compare the amount of sugar used in each recipe.
5 Compare the price of packet custard, egg custard and tinned custard per pint.

▶ ## FOLLOW UP

The care required to prevent custard from curdling must be the focal point of this exercise. All custards should have been examined to establish texture, colour and thickness.

Work out the nutritional value of both custards. Discuss occasions when an egg custard can be a more beneficial addition to a meal than a packet custard.

Look up the digestion of protein.

Find out which members of the community would be most likely to benefit from egg custard in their diet. List dishes which could have egg custard sauce as an accompaniment.

TEACHER'S NOTES

The theory of coagulation of protein in eggs, and the resulting separation if excess heat is used, must be the most important aspects of this assignment.

Double boilers, porringers or makeshift boilers, produced by standing bowls inside pans of hot water, should be investigated. Mention could be made of other foods cooked by this method, e.g., lemon curd.

The use of egg custard as a nutritional booster for invalids and infants should be discussed together with the possibility of adding various flavours to tempt those with poor appetites or those who actively dislike custard-type dishes.

ASSIGNMENT 36

Foods cooked in a microwave oven are often pale and uninteresting with little eye appeal. Various methods of improving the appearance of microwaved food have been devised with some success.

Prepare a batch of plain scones and devise three different ways of making them look more attractive after cooking in a microwave oven. Bake two or three scones from the mixture in a conventional oven for comparison.

▶ ## PREPARATION

1 Look up the basic recipe for a scone mixture.

2 Make sure that this recipe is suitable for microwaving by checking the handbook for your particular cooker.

3 Find out which browning methods are available.

▶ ## PRACTICAL

1 Make up the scone mixture and cook as stated in assignment.

2 Serve scones to class without letting them know what methods of browning have been used.

3 Get class to vote on which method has the most eye appeal.

▶ ## FOLLOW UP

1 Class discussion on the various methods used. Each member reporting to the class on what they did to make the scones look more attractive.

2 Collate results and see which method gets the most votes overall.

TEACHER'S NOTES

A lot of the work in this assignment will hinge on the type of microwave oven being used. If, for example, the oven has a built in browner then the results will be different from those using browning methods recommended for less sophisticated ovens.

Some pupils may be acquainted with browning dishes or the use of a radiant grill, but few may have heard of or used paint-on browning devices. It may be interesting to observe how many different methods are used within the class.

In the assessment session at the end of the practical lesson, pupils could be asked to decide which methods had been used in each batch.

The difference between the 'artificial' browning and natural brownings can be discussed and the end result, including the added cost of each, assessed.

It would be interesting to hold a tasting session—perhaps blindfold—to see if any of these variations could be detected. This is an exercise which would be suitable at any stage in the course and would provide a little light relief at the end of a lesson.

A mention of the necessity of looking after microwave ovens carefully to reduce the risk of leakage is a very important part of the lesson.

ASSIGNMENT 37

Your school is having a summer fete and you are asked to make some toffee to sell on the sweet stall. Prepare a tray of toffee which can be broken up and sold in 50 g packets on the day. In addition make a half quantity of the same recipe into small toffee cakes which can be decorated to attract children.

► ## PREPARATION

1 Look up the recipe for toffee.

2 Check to see how much this recipe will make.

3 Multiply the quantities so that you will have a few packets made at one boiling.

4 Find out how to use a sugar thermometer.

5 Decide how brittle your toffee must be to be broken up for sale.

6 Consider the most suitable economical way of wrapping the toffee for sale.

7 Devise methods of decorating the toffee cakes.

► ## PRACTICAL

1 Prepare the toffee in suitable trays and leave to cool.

2 When cold, break up, weigh into portions and package the toffee.

3 Make and decorate toffee cakes.

► ## FOLLOW UP

1 Find out the price of a similar type of toffee so that you can cost your toffee for sale.

2 Discuss the problems arising from making toffee.

3 Consider the dangers involved in the preparation of sugar products.

4 Think about other ways in which toffee could be presented for sale at a school fete, e.g., toffee apples.

TEACHER'S NOTES

This is a lovely assignment for the end of term when theory becomes quite pleasant and interesting. However the high temperatures involved can make this a very hazardous assignment unless it is carefully monitored.

Accurate measurement of the temperature on a sugar thermometer is essential and the boiling point of sugar must be emphasised.

Theory of the production of sugar at all its stages, as well as its hazards in the diet, can be discussed at this stage.

Correct packaging, costing and hygiene requirements are an essential part of this project.

A further exercise could be the production of chocolate caramel shortbread, which would reinforce the preparation and cooking of shortbread as well as the production of soft toffee and the melting of chocolate.

Sugar-related diseases can be discussed at this stage.

ASSIGNMENT 38

Fresh white breadcrumbs are often used in a variety of recipes, but it is not always easy to buy them ready to use so they must be home-made.

Decide upon three different ways of producing crumbs from a small uncut white loaf and illustrate three ways in which they can be used in cooking.

▶ PREPARATION

1 Using the equipment normally found in your HE room, decide which methods you wish to use.

2 Select the recipes which show the different uses of breadcrumbs.

3 Make out a time plan to fit the length of the lesson.

4 Prepare a chart which will show your findings on which method of making breadcrumbs proved to be best.

5 Discuss difference between breadcrumbs and raspings.

6 Try to find a store in your area which sells breadcrumbs.

▶ PRACTICAL

1 Prepare the breadcrumbs and write up findings on the prepared chart.

2 Prepare, cook and serve chosen dishes.

3 Write briefly to say how the breadcrumbs were incorporated into the separate dishes.

▶ FOLLOW UP

1 Discuss the methods of breadcrumb preparation and, where possible, compare them with others available.

2 Compare time taken by each method.

3 Look at recipes which require breadcrumbs and find out how many more there are than those chosen.

4 See how the breadcrumbs contribute to the food value of each dish.

5 Look at some similar dishes made using brown breadcrumbs and comment on appearance.

TEACHER'S NOTES

This assignment may require a great deal of preparation before the lesson since many pupils may not be conversant with the use of breadcrumbs in cooking or may even confuse breadcrumbs with 'raspings' or 'golden' crumbs. A selection of these on display may be useful.

Pupils may work in groups of 3 and each make up one dish if time is limited.

With lower school pupils or those of very limited ability, the recipes can be provided and may be as simple as necessary to provide a suitable end product, e.g., eggs au gratin. In this way even the younger pupils can participate in an investigatory exercise which may otherwise be too difficult. More advanced students should have no difficulty in preparing the whole assignment.

ASSIGNMENT 39

Canned baked beans are a very popular snack food with all age groups and they can also be used as a vegetable to add fibre to main course dishes. The cans are sold in a variety of sizes and the prices vary considerably.

Using only one brand, compare the prices and the quantities of three different sized cans and decide which is the most economical purchase for:

    a an elderly couple on a limited budget,
    b a student living in a bed-sit with no fridge,
    c a family with two teenage boys.

Prepare, cook and serve a main course dish which could have baked beans served as an accompaniment or which incorporates baked beans.

► PREPARATION

1 Visit your local supermarket and find out how many different brands of baked beans are on sale.
2 Check the prices and the weight of the contents.
3 Decide which is the cheapest and which the most expensive.
4 Divide into groups with each group choosing a different brand.
5 Look up recipes which will be suitable for your assignment.
6 Discuss situations when baked beans could be a valuable store cupboard commodity, e.g., camping, holidays.
7 Work out various ways of assessing the contents of the cans, e.g.
    a drain and measure sauce and then weigh remainder of contents,
    b weigh contents out of the can.
8 Look at the list of contents on the labels and see how they differ from brand to brand.

► PRACTICAL

1 Measure the contents of the cans according to the methods chosen during the preparation period.
2 Record findings.
3 Prepare, cook and serve the chosen meal.
4 Without divulging the brand names run a class tasting session to decide which brand of beans is most popular.

► *FOLLOW UP*

1   Compare the findings from each group in the class to see which brand or non-brand cans are better value on paper.

2   Discuss flavour.

3   Write an account of your reasons for choosing the particular sized can for each of the given groups.

4   Draw up a bar chart illustrating the findings of the whole class to show the 'best buy', bearing in mind the popularity factor.

TEACHER'S NOTES

Baked beans feature in most households on a fairly regular basis and the brands chosen seem to depend upon preferred tastes as well as cost. In this exercise it will be interesting to note how many students have not actually tried more than one variety.

The measurement of sauce separate from the beans may elicit some surprising results; similarly, the list of ingredients may vary considerably.

Less able pupils may be content to use the beans as a straightforward accompaniment to a main course dish, while the more adventurous may look for exciting ways of incorporating the beans into the dish itself.

With guidance, students may also be able to consider the comparative nutritional value of the cans and apply this knowledge in their choice of dishes, as well as in their reasons for choice of can for each of the groups. However, this is an aspect which is not actually suggested in the assignment and pupils should not be penalised for omitting to consider this side of the investigation.

It is vital that the correct and safe use of can openers should be discussed and demonstrated at the beginning of the lesson.

ASSIGNMENT 40

You are preparing individual apple pies for dessert but have noticed that your cooking apples tend to go brown and their fresh colour is spoiled. Devise different methods of preventing this discoloration.

► ## PREPARATION

1 Find out what causes discoloration in cut fruit.

2 What is the scientific name of this browning?

3 Look at methods of slowing it down or stopping it.

4 Decide which methods would seem to be most suitable for the apples going into your pie.

5 Prepare a time plan for the preparation of the pie, taking into consideration any extra time which may be needed for the preparation of the apple.

► ## PRACTICAL

1 Prepare apples for pie.

2 Divide apples equally among chosen methods of preservation.

3 Leave apples to stand for 15 minutes so that any discoloration which may occur can begin.

4 During this time prepare pastry for pies.

5 Examine each batch of apples for discoloration.

6 Make detailed comments on each batch of apples.

7 Using separate marked pie tins, make each batch of apples into pies.

8 When cooked, cut one pie from each batch in half and compare the colour of the finished product.

► ## FOLLOW UP

1 Make a group list of all the methods used in the prevention of browning.

2 Decide which method produced the best results.

3 Discuss reasons for its success.

4 Consider whether or not this method would work with other fruits or vegetables, e.g., potatoes, avocado pears, aubergines, etc.

TEACHER'S NOTES

An element of scientific investigation can be brought into this assignment depending upon the facilities available. A demonstration lesson using non-toxic chemical browning inhibitors such as campden tablets could be useful for the more able candidates, while the less scientifically minded may be able to cope with lemon juice, salt water or even non-carcinogenic cling film to exclude air in order to prevent browning.

Reasons for browning, and also the loss of vitamin C from cut fruit and vegetables, should be brought into this lesson.

It is important to emphasise that the surfaces not covered during the storage process, e.g., top of apple floating in water, will change colour unless moved constantly to keep the surfaces away from the air.

This is a good lesson for the introduction or recap of the shaping of small individual pies as opposed to large plate pies. It could also be used to reinforce work done on oven temperatures for cooking pastry.